MEZE

Mediterranean-style eating

KÖNEMANN

Meze on the Menu

The open air and sunshine inspires us all to entertain outside. While the trusty barbecue is a reliable standby, it's good to tempt our tastebuds with something a little different from time to time.

WHAT IS MEZE?

Combine the rich colours and textures that are typical of Mediterranean countries, relaxing with good friends, cool drinks and dappled sunshine and you're nearly there. Meze is more than a style of food—it's a unique eating experience, a celebration of flavours from Greece, Turkey and the Middle East.

The literal translation from Greek is 'tasty morsels' that are designed to whet your appetite before a main meal. But more and more, we are finding that meze platters make a simply magnificent meal in their own right. There are no rules to tell you how to put together a meze platter—you can be as adventurous as you like.

OILS AIN'T OILS

Much of the preparation for a meze platter can be done in advance as the food can be served cold, warm or hot. This means you can relax with your friends as you offer them such temptations as kebabs, dolmades, bean dishes, dips and breads, marinated vegetables and seafood. And your guests don't need to

feel guilty if they squeeze in 'just one more' as Mediterranean cuisine is very healthy, predominantly made up of fish, vegetables, pulses and rice, and only small amounts of red meat and dairy products. Olive oil features in almost every dish. It complements the flavours of the other ingredients, and adds a little fruitiness of its own, without being overpowering. Better still, it has no cholesterol, which contributes to Mediterranean countries having a low incidence of heart disease.

MEZE—THE COMPLETE DINING EXPERIENCE

Meze is not restricted to finger food. Soups, salads and breads can help make it a full and satisfying meal. If you are planning to serve meze to four people as a main meal, a rough guide would be to allow about two recipes per person (giving you a total of eight different dishes) served with plenty of crusty bread. Tradition suggests that all the meze plates should be brought out together, allowing you and your guests to have a relaxed meal, picking at a variety of dishes,

but this is entirely up to you. Chilled retsina is the perfect accompaniment to the rich flavours of a meze platter. Or, for something completely different, try the unique licorice flavour of ouzo. Served straight or with a little iced water, it is a delicious and authentic accompaniment.

From left to right: Souvlakia; Greek village salad; Dill, garlic and orange marinated olives; Tabbouleh; Vegetarian dolmades; cubes of Greek feta.

Meze

S elect a few of our tempting recipes to make a meze platter that will delight (not to mention impress) your friends.

Grilled lamb kofta

Preparation time:
  20 minutes +
  1 hour soaking
Total cooking time:
  10 minutes
Makes 8

400 g lean lamb mince
1 tablespoon chopped
  fresh flat-leaf parsley
1 teaspoon ground
  cumin
2 tablespoons chopped
  fresh coriander
pinch of cayenne pepper
2 cloves garlic, crushed
$^{1}/_{2}$ teaspoon dried mint
$^{3}/_{4}$ cup (185 g) thick
  Greek-style yoghurt

1. Soak eight 15 cm skewers in water for 1 hour, or until they sink, to ensure that they don't burn during cooking.
2. Combine the lamb mince, parsley, cumin, coriander, cayenne pepper, half the garlic and $^{1}/_{2}$ teaspoon salt in a bowl and knead the mixture by hand for a few minutes until smooth and the mixture leaves the side of the bowl.
3. Divide the mixture into 16 portions. With cool, clean hands, roll each portion into a ball. Thread two balls onto each prepared skewer, moulding each ball into an oval shape 4–5 cm long.
4. Combine the dried mint, yoghurt and remaining clove of garlic in a bowl. Season with salt and pepper.
5. Heat a lightly oiled barbecue hot plate until hot or heat a grill to its highest setting. Cook the kofta for about 6 minutes, turning once. Serve hot with yoghurt mint sauce.

NUTRITION PER KOFTA
Protein 12 g; Fat 2.5 g; Carbohydrate 1 g; Dietary Fibre 0 g; Cholesterol 35 mg; 325 kJ (80 cal)

Grilled lamb kofta

Cauliflower fritters

Preparation time:
15 minutes +
30 minutes standing
Total cooking time:
15 minutes
Serves 4–6

600 g cauliflower
1/2 cup (55 g) besan
flour
2 teaspoons ground
cumin
1 teaspoon ground
coriander
1 teaspoon ground
turmeric
pinch cayenne pepper
1 egg, lightly beaten
1 egg yolk
oil, for deep-frying

1. Cut the cauliflower
into bite-sized florets.
Sift the flour and spices
into a bowl, then stir in
1/2 teaspoon salt.
2. Lightly whisk 1/4 cup
(60 ml) water, the
beaten egg and egg yolk
in a jug. Make a well
in the centre of the dry
ingredients and pour
in the egg mixture,
mixing with a whisk
until smooth. Stand
for 30 minutes.
3. Fill a deep pan one-
third full of oil and heat
until a cube of bread
dropped into the oil
browns in 15 seconds.

Holding the florets by
the stem, dip them into
the batter, allowing the
excess batter to drain
back into the bowl.
Deep-fry in batches for
3–4 minutes, or until
puffed and browned.
Drain, sprinkle with
salt and serve hot.

NUTRITION PER SERVE (6)
Protein 5 g; Fat 5 g;
Carbohydrate 7 g; Dietary
Fibre 3 g; Cholesterol
60 mg; 390 kJ (95 cal)

Note: Besan flour is
chickpea flour and is
available at health
food stores.

Stuffed zucchini flowers

Preparation time:
1 hour 20 minutes
+ 1 hour standing
Total cooking time:
10 minutes
Makes 24

1 1/2 cups (185 g)
plain flour
7 g dry yeast or
15 g compressed
fresh yeast
24 zucchini with flowers
50 g kefalotyri cheese
20 g (8) anchovy fillets
oil, for deep-frying

1. Sift the flour and
1/4 teaspoon salt into a
bowl and make a well

in the centre. Whisk
the yeast and 1 1/4 cups
(315 ml) warm water
in a bowl until dissolved
and pour into the well.
Gradually stir with the
whisk to form a thick,
tacky batter. Cover
with plastic wrap and
leave in a warm place
for 1 hour, or until
frothy. Do not stir.
2. Gently open the
zucchini flowers and
remove the centre
stamens. Wash and
drain dry. Cut the
cheese into 1 cm cubes.
Drain the anchovy
fillets and cut into
1 1/2 cm pieces.
3. Put a cube of cheese
and a piece of anchovy
into the centre of each
flower. Re-form the
petals around them.
Fill a deep pan one-
third full of oil and heat
until a cube of bread
dropped into the oil
browns in 15 seconds.
Dip the flowers into the
batter, turning to coat
and drain off the excess.
Deep-fry in batches for
1–2 minutes, or until
puffed and lightly
brown. Drain. Serve hot.

NUTRITION PER SERVE
Protein 2 g; Fat 1.5 g;
Carbohydrate 5.5 g; Dietary
Fibre 0.5 g; Cholesterol
2.5 mg; 195 kJ (45 cal)

Note: Kefalotyri is a
pale hard sheep's milk
cheese. If unavailable,
Parmesan or pecorino
can be substituted.

Cauliflower fritters (top) and
Stuffed zucchini flowers

Vegetarian dolmades

Preparation time:
1 hour + cooling time
Total cooking time:
1 hour 5 minutes
Makes 20–25

1/2 *cup (125 ml) olive oil*
6 spring onions, chopped
3/4 *cup (150 g) long-grain rice*
1/4 *cup (15 g) chopped fresh mint*
2 tablespoons chopped fresh dill
2/3 *cup (170 ml) lemon juice*
1/4 *cup (35 g) currants*
1/4 *cup (40 g) pine nuts*
240 g (about 50) packaged vine leaves
2 tablespoons olive oil, extra

1. Heat the oil in a pan. Add the spring onion and cook over medium heat for 1 minute. Stir in the rice, mint, dill, half the lemon juice, and season to taste. Add 1 cup (250 ml) water and bring to the boil, then reduce the heat, cover and simmer for 20 minutes. Remove the lid, fork through the currants and pine nuts, cover with a paper towel, then the lid and leave to cool.
2. Rinse the vine leaves under water and gently separate. Drain, then dry on paper towels. Trim any thick stems with scissors. Line the base of a 20 cm pan (with a lid) with any torn or misshapen leaves. Choose the larger leaves for filling and use smaller leaves to patch up any gaps.
3. Place each leaf shiny-side-down. Spoon a tablespoon of filling into the centre, bring in the sides and roll up tightly from the stem end. Place seam-side-down with the stem end closest to you in the base of the pan, tightly in a single layer.
4. Pour in the rest of the lemon juice, the extra oil and about 3/4 cup (185 ml) water to just cover the dolmades. Cover with an inverted plate and place a tin on the plate to firmly compress the dolmades. Cover with the lid.
5. Bring to the boil, then reduce the heat and simmer for 45 minutes. Allow to cool in the pan. Serve at room temperature.

NUTRITION PER SERVE
Protein 1.5 g; Fat 7.5 g; Carbohydrate 5.5 g; Dietary Fibre 0 g; Cholesterol 0 mg; 380 kJ (90 cal)

Note: The dolmades will store, covered in the cooking liquid, in the refrigerator for up to 2 weeks.

Vegetarian dolmades

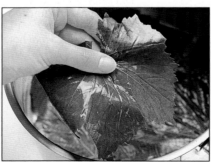

Line the base of the pan with any torn or misshapen leaves.

Trim any thick stems from the vine leaves with kitchen scissors.

Bring in the sides of the leaves and roll up tightly from the stem end.

Put the dolmades seam-side-down into the pan, fitting them tightly in a single layer.

Baked eggplant

Preparation time:
  40 minutes +
  30 minutes standing
Total cooking time:
  1 hour 20 minutes
Serves 6

6 slender eggplants
1/3 cup (80 ml) olive oil
2 onions, halved and sliced
2 cloves garlic, crushed
1 ripe tomato, finely chopped
1 tablespoon finely chopped fresh flat-leaf parsley
1 teaspoon chopped fresh dill
1/4 teaspoon ground cinnamon
1 teaspoon paprika
1/4 teaspoon sugar
2 tablespoons currants
1 tomato, extra, halved, grated and skin discarded

1. Make two deep cuts lengthways in each eggplant to make pockets without cutting all the way through. Hold open the pockets and sprinkle generously with salt. Leave in a colander for 30 minutes, then rinse well and drain on paper towels.
2. Heat half the oil in a frying pan, add the onion and cook over low heat for 20 minutes, or until very soft. Add the garlic and cook for a further 5 minutes. Increase the heat to medium and add the tomato, parsley, dill, cinnamon, paprika, sugar and currants. Cook for 10 minutes, or until thick and pulpy. Taste before seasoning. Preheat the oven to moderate 180°C (350°F/Gas 4).
3. Heat the remaining oil over medium heat in a large frying pan and brown the eggplant all over for about 10 minutes, or until the skin has changed colour and the eggplants are soft. Drain on paper towels.
4. Put the eggplants in an ovenproof dish large enough to fit them in a single layer. Carefully open the pockets and spoon in the filling (or use your fingers). Spoon the grated tomato around the eggplant and bake, covered, for 20 minutes. Uncover and bake for a further 15 minutes. Delicious served warm or at room temperature.

NUTRITION PER SERVE
Protein 2.5 g; Fat 13 g; Carbohydrate 6.5 g; Dietary Fibre 4 g; Cholesterol 0 mg; 630 kJ (150 cal)

Baked eggplant (top) and Fried chickpeas

Fried chickpeas

Preparation time:
  30 minutes +
  overnight soaking
Total cooking time:
  15 minutes
Serves 5

285 g dried chickpeas
oil, for deep-frying
1/2 teaspoon paprika
1/4 teaspoon cayenne pepper

1. Soak the chickpeas in plenty of cold water overnight. Drain well.
2. Fill a deep pan one-third full of oil and heat until a cube of bread dropped into the oil browns in 15 seconds. Deep-fry half the chickpeas for 3 minutes. Drain and repeat with the rest of the chickpeas. Partially cover the deep fryer as some beans may pop. Don't leave the oil unattended.
3. Deep-fry the chickpeas again in batches for 3 minutes each batch, or until browned. Drain. Season the paprika with salt and cayenne pepper, and sprinkle over the chickpeas while still hot. Cool before serving.

NUTRITION PER SERVE
Protein 3.5 g; Fat 5 g; Carbohydrate 7.5 g; Dietary Fibre 2.5 g; Cholesterol 0 mg; 375 kJ (90 cal)

Mushrooms in red wine

Preparation time:
  15 minutes +
  overnight marinating
Total cooking time:
  30 minutes
Serves 6

400 g cap mushrooms
20 g butter
1 tablespoon olive oil
4 small brown pickling
  onions, quartered
1 bay leaf
1/2 cup (125 ml) dry
  red wine
1 tablespoon lemon
  juice
1 tablespoon chopped
  fresh dill
2 tablespoons chopped
  fresh coriander

1. Trim the stalks and halve the mushrooms.
2. Melt the butter and oil in a large heavy-based pan. When foaming, add the onions, and toss over medium heat for 2 minutes, or until starting to brown. Add the mushrooms. Cook for 2–3 minutes, or until they are beginning to soften and brown.
3. Add the bay leaf, wine and lemon juice. Bring to the boil, then reduce the heat to low and simmer, covered, for 25 minutes, or until the mushrooms are tender. Remove the bay leaf and stir in the dill and coriander. Taste before seasoning with salt and cracked black pepper. Transfer to an airtight container and marinate the mushrooms in the refrigerator overnight or for up to 2 days. Delicious served hot or cold.

NUTRITION PER SERVE
Protein 2.5 g; Fat 3 g;
Carbohydrate 2.5 g; Dietary
Fibre 2 g; Cholesterol
8.5 mg; 260 kJ (60 cal)

Zucchini patties

Preparation time:
  20 minutes
Total cooking time:
  15 minutes
Makes 16

2 medium zucchini,
  grated
1 small onion, grated
1/4 cup (30 g) self-
  raising flour
1/3 cup (35 g) grated
  kefalotyri cheese or
  Parmesan
1 tablespoon chopped
  fresh mint
2 teaspoons chopped
  fresh parsley
pinch ground nutmeg
1/4 cup (25 g) dry
  breadcrumbs
1 egg
olive oil, for shallow-
  frying

1. Put the zucchini and onion into the centre of a clean tea towel, twist as tightly as possible and squeeze dry. Combine the zucchini, onion, flour, cheese, mint, parsley, nutmeg, breadcrumbs and egg in a large bowl. Season well with salt and cracked black pepper, and mix with clean hands to a stiff mixture that clumps together.
2. Heat the shallow-frying oil in a large pan over medium heat. Drop level tablespoons of the mixture into the pan and shallow-fry for 2–3 minutes, or until well browned all over. Drain well on paper towels and serve hot. The patties can be served plain sprinkled with salt or are delicious served with tzatziki (see page 49).

NUTRITION PER SERVE
Protein 2.5 g; Fat 2 g;
Carbohydrate 3 g; Dietary
Fibre 0.5 g; Cholesterol
13 mg; 165 kJ (40 cal)

Note: Kefalotyri and kefalograviera are pale hard sheep's milk cheeses originating in Greece. In this recipe, Parmesan or pecorino cheeses may be substituted.

*Mushrooms in red wine (top) and
Zucchini patties*

With clean hands, roll the wheat mixture into a smooth sausage shape.

Make a hole with your forefinger and gently work into a shell.

Kibbeh

Preparation time:
45 minutes + 2 hours
refrigeration
Total cooking time:
25 minutes
Makes 15

1¹/3 cups (235 g) fine
burghul wheat
150 g lean lamb, chopped
1 onion, grated
2 tablespoons plain flour
1 teaspoon ground allspice

Filling
2 teaspoons olive oil
1 small onion, finely
chopped
100 g lean lamb mince
¹/2 teaspoon ground
allspice
¹/2 teaspoon ground
cinnamon
¹/3 cup (80 ml) beef stock
2 tablespoons pine nuts
2 tablespoons chopped
fresh mint
oil, for deep-frying

1. Cover the wheat with boiling water and leave for 5 minutes. Drain in a colander, pressing well to remove the water. Spread on paper towels to absorb any moisture.
2. Process the wheat, lamb, onion, flour and allspice until a fine paste forms. Season well. Refrigerate for 1 hour.
3. To make the filling, heat the oil in a frying pan, add the onion and cook over low heat for 3 minutes, or until soft. Add the mince, allspice and cinnamon, and cook, stirring, over high heat, for 3 minutes. Add the stock and cook, partially covered, over low heat for 6 minutes, or until the mince is soft. Roughly chop the pine nuts and stir in with the mint. Season well with salt and cracked pepper, then transfer to a bowl and allow to cool.

4. Shape 2 tablespoons of the wheat mixture into a sausage shape 6 cm long. Dip your hands in cold water, and, with your finger, make a long hole through the centre and gently work your finger around to make a shell. Fill with 2 teaspoons of the filling and seal, moulding it into a torpedo shape. Smooth over any cracks with your fingers. Place on a foil-lined tray and refrigerate, uncovered, for 1 hour.
5. Fill a deep pan one-third full of oil and heat until a cube of bread dropped into the oil browns in 15 seconds. Deep-fry the kibbeh in batches for 2–3 minutes, or until browned. Drain on paper towels. Serve hot.

NUTRITION PER SERVE
*Protein 4.5 g; Fat 3 g;
Carbohydrate 10 g; Dietary
Fibre 2 g; Cholesterol
6.5 mg; 350 kJ (85 cal)*

Kibbeh

Spoon 2 teaspoons of the filling into the centre and close the open end.

Mould into a smooth torpedo shape with pointed ends.

Meatballs

Preparation time:
  25 minutes +
  30 minutes chilling
Total cooking time:
  20 minutes
Makes about 28

115 g (4 slices) white
  bread, crusts removed
150 g pork mince
150 g veal mince
1 tablespoon chopped
  fresh flat-leaf parsley
1 tablespoon chopped
  fresh mint
1 onion, grated
1/2 teaspoon ground
  cumin
1 egg
1/4 cup (25 g) grated
  kefalotyri or Parmesan
1/2 cup (60 g) plain
  flour
olive oil, for shallow-
  frying

1. Cover the bread
with water in a bowl,
and squeeze out as
much water as possible.
Place in a large bowl
with the mince, parsley,
mint, onion, cumin,
egg and cheese. Season.
Knead the mixture by
hand for 2–3 minutes
until smooth. Cover
and refrigerate for
30 minutes.
2. Put the flour in a
shallow dish. With
wet hands, roll level
tablespoons of mixture
into balls. Heat the
shallow-frying oil over
medium heat. Toss the
meatballs in the flour.
Shallow-fry in batches
for 3–5 minutes, or
until the meatballs are
browned and cooked
through. Drain on
paper towels. Serve hot.

NUTRITION PER MEATBALL
Protein 3.5 g; Fat 2 g;
Carbohydrate 3.5 g; Dietary
Fibre 0 g; Cholesterol
10 mg; 195 kJ (45 cal)

Mussels Saganaki

Preparation time:
  45 minutes
Total cooking time:
  25 minutes
Serves 6

750 g small black
  mussels
1/2 cup (125 ml) dry
  white wine
3 sprigs fresh thyme
1 bay leaf
1 tablespoon olive oil
1 large onion, finely
  chopped
1 clove garlic, finely
  chopped
420 g ripe tomatoes,
  halved, grated and
  skin discarded
2 tablespoons tomato
  paste
1/2 teaspoon sugar
1 tablespoon red wine
  vinegar
70 g feta, crumbled
1 teaspoon fresh thyme
  leaves

1. Scrub the mussels
and remove the beards.
Discard any open
mussels. Bring the wine,
thyme and bay leaf to
the boil in a large pan,
add the mussels and
cook for 5 minutes.
Pour the mussel liquid
through a strainer into
a heatproof jug and
reserve. Discard any
unopened mussels.
Remove one half shell
from each mussel and
discard.
2. Heat the oil in a pan,
add the onion and cook
over medium heat for
3 minutes. Add the garlic
and cook for 1 minute,
or until fragrant. Pour
in the reserved mussel
liquid, increase the heat
and bring it to the boil,
then boil for 2 minutes,
or until almost dry.
Add the tomatoes,
tomato paste and
sugar, then reduce the
heat and simmer for
5 minutes. Add the
vinegar and simmer
for 5 minutes.
3. Add the mussels
and cook over medium
heat for 1 minute, or
until heated through.
Top with the crumbled
feta and thyme leaves.
Serve hot.

NUTRITION PER SERVE
Protein 5 g; Fat 9 g;
Carbohydrate 4 g; Dietary
Fibre 1.5 g; Cholesterol
10 mg; 891 kJ (210 cal)

Meatballs (top) and
Mussels Saganaki

Felafel

Preparation time:
  20 minutes
  + overnight soaking
  + 2 hours chilling
Total cooking time:
  15 minutes
Makes about 16

250 g dried chickpeas
4 spring onions, chopped
2 cloves garlic, crushed
1/2 cup (15 g) chopped
  fresh flat-leaf parsley
1/4 cup (15 g) chopped
  fresh mint
1/2 cup (25 g) chopped
  fresh coriander
1/4 teaspoon cayenne
  pepper
2 teaspoons ground
  cumin
2 teaspoons ground
  coriander
1/2 teaspoon baking
  powder
oil, for deep-frying

1. Cover the chickpeas with plenty of cold water and leave overnight. Drain well.
2. Combine the chickpeas, spring onions, garlic, parsley, mint, coriander, cayenne pepper, cumin, ground coriander, baking powder and 1 teaspoon salt. Process in batches for 30–40 seconds, or until finely chopped and the mixture is sticky and holds together. Refrigerate, uncovered, for at least 2 hours.
3. Press 2 tablespoons of mixture together in the palm of your hand and form into a patty. Fill a deep pan one-third full of oil and heat until a cube of bread dropped into the oil browns in 15 seconds. Deep-fry the felafel in batches for 3–4 minutes, or until well browned. Drain on paper towels and serve hot with hummus (see page 49).

NUTRITION PER FELAFEL
Protein 3 g; Fat 3.5 g;
Carbohydrate 6 g; Dietary
Fibre 2 g; Cholesterol
0 mg; 265 kJ (65 cal)

Labneh

Preparation time:
  20 minutes +
  4 days chilling
Total cooking time:
  Nil
Makes 12

2 cups (500 g) thick
  Greek-style yoghurt
2 teaspoons sea salt
1 tablespoon dried
  oregano
2 teaspoons dried
  thyme leaves
1 bay leaf
1 1/3 cups (350 ml)
  olive oil

1. Fold a 60 cm x 30 cm piece of muslin in half to make a 30 cm square.
2. Combine the yoghurt, salt and 1 teaspoon black pepper in a bowl. Line a bowl with the muslin and spoon the mixture into the centre. Bring the corners together and, using a piece of kitchen string, tie as closely as possible to the yoghurt, leaving a loop at the end. Thread the loop through the handle of a wooden spoon and hang over a bowl to drain in the refrigerator for 3 days.
3. Combine the oregano and thyme in a shallow bowl. Pour half the oil into a 2 cup (500 ml) jar and add the bay leaf.
4. Roll level tablespoons of the mixture into balls. Toss in the combined herbs and place into the jar of oil. Pour in the remaining oil to cover the balls completely, seal and refrigerate for at least 1 day. Serve at room temperature.

NUTRITION PER LABNEH
Protein 2 g; Fat 6 g;
Carbohydrate 2 g; Dietary
Fibre 0 g; Cholesterol
3 mg; 240 kJ (57 cal)

Note: Labneh can be made up to 2 months ahead and kept in the refrigerator. The oil will turn white and set in the refrigerator, but will return to liquid at room temperature.

Felafel (top) with Labneh

Chorizo salad with mint

Preparation time:
30 minutes
Total cooking time:
25 minutes
Serves 6

5 chorizo sausages
1/2 cup (125 ml) red
  wine vinegar
3 tablespoons caster
  sugar
1 large red onion,
  thinly sliced
1 tablespoon shredded
  fresh mint

1. Preheat the oven to moderate 180°C (350°F/Gas 4).
2. Prick the chorizo sausages with a fork and roast in the oven for 10–20 minutes, or until cooked through. Set aside to cool.
3. In a large pan with a tight-fitting lid, combine the red wine vinegar and the sugar. Stir over low heat until the sugar dissolves. Add the onion, cover, and cook over low heat for 2 minutes. Remove from the heat and allow to cool. Drain, reserving 1/4 cup (60 ml) of the cooking liquid.
4. Slice the chorizo sausage into bite-sized slices and toss in a bowl with the drained onions and shredded mint. Serve warm or cold, drizzled with the reserved liquid.

NUTRITION PER SERVE
Protein 8 g; Fat 15 g; Carbohydrate 5.5 g; Dietary Fibre 0.5 g; Cholesterol 40 mg; 940 kJ (225 cal)

Barbecued quail

Preparation time:
40 minutes +
3 hours chilling
Total cooking time:
10 minutes
Serves 6

6 quail
1 cup (250 ml) dry red
  wine
2 sticks celery, including
  tops, chopped
1 carrot, chopped
1 small onion, chopped
1 bay leaf, torn into
  small pieces
1 teaspoon allspice
1 teaspoon dried thyme
2 cloves garlic, crushed
2 tablespoons olive oil
2 tablespoons lemon
  juice
1 lemon, cut into
  wedges for serving

1. To prepare the quail, use poultry shears to cut down either side of the backbone, then discard the backbone. Remove the innards, wash the inside of the quail and pat dry with paper towels. Place the quail breast-side-up on the bench, open out flat and gently press to flatten. Using poultry shears, cut in half through the breast then cut each half in half again into the thigh and drumstick piece and breast and wing piece.
2. In a non-metallic bowl, combine the wine, celery, carrot, onion, bay leaf and allspice. Add the quail and stir to coat. Cover and refrigerate for 3 hours, or preferably overnight, stirring occasionally. Drain and sprinkle with thyme, salt and pepper.
3. Whisk the garlic, oil and lemon juice in a small bowl.
4. Heat a lightly oiled barbecue plate until hot or heat a grill to its highest setting. Reduce the heat to medium and cook the quail breast pieces for 4–5 minutes on each side and the drumstick pieces for 3 minutes each side, or until tender and cooked through. Brush frequently with the lemon mixture. Serve hot with lemon.

NUTRITION PER SERVE
Protein 7 g; Fat 12.5 g; Carbohydrate 2 g; Dietary Fibre 1 g; Cholesterol 0 mg; 1150 kJ (275 cal)

Chorizo salad with mint (top) and Barbecued quail

Put the cod in a large bowl, cover with water and soak for 8–12 hours.

When the fish is cool enough to handle, remove the skin and bones.

Bacalao croquettes with skordalia

Preparation time:
50 minutes +
8–12 hours soaking
Total cooking time:
55 minutes
Makes 24

400 g dried salt cod or
bacalao (see Note)
300 g floury potatoes,
unpeeled
1 small (25 g) brown
pickling onion,
grated
2 tablespoons chopped
fresh flat-leaf parsley
1 egg, lightly beaten
oil, for deep-frying

Skordalia
250 g floury potatoes,
unpeeled
2 cloves garlic, crushed
1 tablespoon white
wine vinegar
2 tablespoons olive
oil

1. Soak the cod in a large bowl covered with water for 8–12 hours, changing the water three times. This will remove the excess salt from the cod. Drain on paper towels.
2. To make the skordalia, boil or steam the potatoes until tender, remove the peel and mash. Allow to cool and add the garlic, vinegar and oil. Season with salt and cracked black pepper, then mix with a fork. Set aside.
3. Put the cod in a pan, cover with water, bring to the boil and cook for 15 minutes. Drain well and dry on paper towels. When cool enough to handle, remove the skin and bones from the cod and flake with your fingers into a bowl. Meanwhile, boil or steam the potatoes until tender, remove the peel and mash.

4. Add the mashed potato to the cod with the onion, parsley, egg and 1/2 teaspoon cracked pepper. Mix well with a wooden spoon to form a thick mixture. Taste before seasoning with salt.
5 Fill a deep pan one-third full of oil and heat until a cube of bread dropped into the oil browns in 15 seconds. Drop level tablespoons of the mixture into the oil and cook in batches for 2–3 minutes, or until well browned. Drain. Serve hot with skordalia.

NUTRITION PER SERVE
Protein 5 g; Fat 4 g;
Carbohydrate 3.5 g; Dietary
Fibre 1 g; Cholesterol
75 mg; 365 kJ (85 cal)

Note: Dried bacalao or salted cod is available at delicatessens or fish markets. The skordalia can be made up to 4 days ahead and kept covered in the refrigerator until needed.

Bacalao croquettes with skordalia

Use your fingers to flake the cod into a bowl and set aside.

Drop level tablespoons of the mixture into the hot oil and cook until browned.

Chicken rolls

Preparation time:
1 hour 15 minutes
Total cooking time:
1 hour 5 minutes
Makes about 40

60 g butter
1 large onion, chopped
2 cloves garlic, crushed
2 tablespoons plain
    flour
1/2 cup (125 ml)
    chicken stock
1/2 cup (125 ml) milk
1 large barbecued
    chicken, skin removed
    and flesh shredded
1/4 cup (25 g) grated
    Parmesan
2 teaspoons fresh
    thyme leaves
1/4 cup (25 g) dry
    breadcrumbs
2 eggs, lightly beaten
13 sheets filo pastry,
    cut into thirds
    crossways
140 g butter, extra,
    melted

1. Melt the butter in a pan and add the onion. Cook over low heat for 12 minutes, or until soft, stirring occasionally. Increase the heat to medium–high and add the garlic. Cook, stirring for 1 minute, then add the flour and stir over heat for a further 1 minute. Remove from the heat and gradually add the stock and milk, stirring constantly until smooth. Return to high heat and bring to the boil, stirring constantly until the sauce boils and thickens. Boil for 1 minute, then remove from the heat and add the chicken, Parmesan, thyme, breadcrumbs, salt and pepper. Cool, then stir in the eggs.
2. Preheat the oven to hot 220°C (425°F/ Gas 7). Lightly grease three baking trays.
3. Put one piece of filo pastry on the bench with the short end closest to you (cover the remaining pieces with a damp tea towel). Brush with the extra melted butter and place a level tablespoon of chicken mixture on the base end closest to you. Fold in the sides, brush along the length with butter and roll up tightly to form a roll 7–8 cm long. Put onto the baking tray and brush the top with some of the butter. Repeat with the remaining filo, butter and chicken mixture.
4. Bake for 15 minutes in the top half of the oven until well browned. Serve hot.

NUTRITION PER ROLL
*Protein 4 g; Fat 5.5 g;
Carbohydrate 3 g; Dietary
Fibre 0 g; Cholesterol
35 mg; 335 kJ (80 cal)*

Pickled baby cos

Preparation time:
20 minutes + cooling
Total cooking time:
5 minutes
Serves 6

1/4 cup (60 ml)
    balsamic vinegar
1/4 cup (60 ml) olive oil
1 teaspoon soft brown
    sugar
3 baby cos (see Note)

1. In a bowl combine the vinegar, oil and sugar.
2. Peel off the outer layers of lettuce to reach the heart of each cos. Wash thoroughly under running water. Cut the hearts in half.
3. Put the cos hearts in a pan of lightly salted boiling water, and simmer for 3 minutes, or until just tender but still in one piece. Drain. Place in a shallow dish, top with the balsamic mixture, and allow to cool before serving.

NUTRITION PER SERVE
*Protein 0 g; Fat 10 g;
Carbohydrate 1 g; Dietary
Fibre 0.5 g; Cholesterol
0 mg; 380 kJ (90 cal)*

Note: If unavailable, choose firm medium-sized cos. Remove about half of the outer leaves to find the heart.

*Chicken rolls (top)
with Pickled baby cos*

Tomato and eggplant borek

Preparation time:
  50 minutes + 1 hour refrigeration
Total cooking time:
  1 hour
Makes 30

75 g butter, melted
1/3 cup (80 ml) olive oil
1 1/2 cups (185 g) plain flour

Filling
250 g tomatoes
2 teaspoons olive oil
1 small onion, chopped
1/2 teaspoon ground cumin
300 g eggplant, cut into 2 cm cubes
2 teaspoons tomato paste
1 tablespoon chopped fresh coriander
1 egg, lightly beaten

1. Put the butter, oil and 1/3 cup (80 ml) water into a bowl. Season well with salt. Gradually add the flour in batches, mixing with a wooden spoon, to form an oily, lumpy dough that leaves the side of the bowl. Knead gently to bring the dough together, cover with plastic wrap and refrigerate for 1 hour.

2. Core the tomatoes and cut a small cross at the base. Plunge into a pan of boiling water and leave for 1 minute. Drain, plunge into cold water, then remove the peel. Halve the tomatoes, squeeze over a bowl to remove the seeds, and finely chop the flesh.
3. Heat the oil in a frying pan, add the onion and cook, stirring, over low heat for 2–3 minutes, or until soft. Add the cumin, cook for 1 minute, then add the eggplant and cook, stirring, for 8–10 minutes, or until the eggplant begins to soften. Stir in the tomato and paste. Cook over medium heat for 15 minutes, or until the mixture becomes dry. Stir occasionally. Season and stir in the coriander. Cool.
4. Preheat the oven to moderate 180°C (350°F/Gas 4). Lightly grease two oven trays.
5. Roll out half the pastry on a lightly floured surface until 2 mm thick. Using an 8 1/2 cm cutter, cut rounds from the pastry. Spoon 2 level teaspoons of the mixture into the centre of each round, lightly brush the edges with water, and fold over the filling,

expelling any air. Press firmly and crimp the edge with a fork to seal. Place on the oven trays and brush with the beaten egg. Bake in the top half of the oven for 25 minutes, or until browned and crisp.

NUTRITION PER BOREK
Protein 1 g; Fat 5 g;
Carbohydrate 5 g; Dietary
Fibre 0.5 g; Cholesterol
12 mg; 295 kJ (70 cal)

Greek village salad

Preparation time:
  20 minutes
Total cooking time: Nil
Serves 6–8

6 tomatoes, cut into thin wedges
1 red onion, cut into thin rings
2 Lebanese cucumbers, sliced
185 g Kalamata olives
200 g feta
1/2 cup (125 ml) extra virgin olive oil
dried oregano, to garnish

1. Combine the tomato, onion, cucumber and olives in a bowl. Season to taste.
2. Break the feta into large pieces and scatter over the top. Top with olive oil and oregano.

NUTRITION PER SERVE (8)
Protein 6.5 g; Fat 20 g;
Carbohydrate 4 g; Dietary
Fibre 2.5 g; Cholesterol
17 mg; 980 kJ (235 cal)

Tomato and eggplant borek (top)
with Greek village salad

Spinach pie

Preparation time:
  50 minutes + 1 hour
  chilling
Total cooking time:
  50 minutes
Makes 16 pieces

2 cups (250 g) plain
  flour
30 g butter, chopped
1/4 cup (60 ml) olive oil
1/2 cup (125 ml) warm
  water

Filling
420 g English spinach
1 leek, white part only,
  halved lengthways
  and thinly sliced
1/4 teaspoon ground
  nutmeg
2 teaspoons chopped
  fresh dill
200 g feta, crumbled
1 tablespoon dry
  breadcrumbs
3 eggs, lightly beaten
2 tablespoons olive
  oil

1. Lightly oil a 28 cm
x 18 cm x 3 cm tin.
2. Sift the flour into
a bowl and stir in
1/2 teaspoon salt.
Using your fingertips,
rub the butter into
the flour until the
mixture resembles fine
breadcrumbs. Pour in
the oil and rub it in by
lifting the flour mixture
onto one hand and
lightly rubbing the
other hand over the top.

The mixture should
clump together. Make a
well in the centre and,
while mixing by hand,
add enough water to
form a firm supple
dough. Knead gently
to bring the dough
together—it may not
be completely smooth.
Cover with plastic wrap
and chill for 1 hour.
3. Trim the bottom
quarter from the
spinach stalks.
Wash and shred the
remaining leaves and
stalks. Pile the spinach
onto a clean tea towel,
twist as tightly as
possible and squeeze
dry. Put into a bowl
with the leek, nutmeg,
dill, feta, breadcrumbs
and 1/2 teaspoon
cracked black pepper.
4. Preheat the oven to
hot 220°C (425°F/
Gas 7). Roll out just
over half the dough on
a lightly floured surface
until large enough to
line the base and sides
of the tin. Lift the
dough into the tin,
pressing evenly over the
base and sides.
5. Add the eggs and oil
to the spinach mixture.
Mix with your hand,
but do not overmix or
the mixture will become
too wet. Spoon into
the pastry-lined tin.
6. Roll out the
remaining pastry on a
lightly floured surface

until large enough to
cover the tin. Lift
onto the tin and press
the two pastry edges
firmly together to seal.
Trim the excess pastry
with a sharp knife
from the outer edge of
the tin, then brush the
top with a little extra
olive oil. Using a sharp
knife, mark into three
strips lengthways and
then diagonally into
diamonds. Make two
or three small slits
through the top layer
of pastry to allow the
steam to escape.
7. Bake the pie for
45–50 minutes in the
centre of the oven, or
until well browned.
Cover with foil if the
pastry is overbrowning.
The pie is cooked if it
slides when you gently
shake the tin. Turn
out onto wire rack to
cool for 10 minutes,
then turn onto a cutting
board or back into tin
to cut into diamonds.
Delicious served warm
or cold.

NUTRITION PER PIECE
*Protein 6 g; Fat 12 g;
Carbohydrate 12 g; Dietary
Fibre 1.5 g; Cholesterol
45 mg; 735 kJ (175 cal)*

Note: The pastry is even
better if it is made the
night before. White
spots on the surface of
the pastry are the oil
setting when cold.

Spinach pie

Meat patties with haloumi filling

Preparation time:
25 minutes +
30 minutes chilling
Total cooking time:
10 minutes
Makes 12

4 slices (125 g) white
bread, crusts removed
350 g lamb or beef
mince
2 teaspoons chopped
fresh flat-leaf parsley
1 1/2 tablespoons
chopped fresh mint
1 small onion, grated
1 egg, lightly beaten
70 g haloumi (see Note)
2 tablespoons plain
flour
olive oil, for shallow-
frying

1. Put the bread in a bowl, cover with water and then squeeze out as much water as possible. Place the bread in a bowl with the mince, parsley, mint, onion, egg, pepper and 1/2 teaspoon salt. Knead the mixture by hand for 2–3 minutes, breaking up the mince and any large pieces of bread with your fingers. The mixture should be smooth and leave the side of the bowl. Cover and refrigerate

for 30 minutes.
2. Cut the haloumi into 12 rectangular pieces, 3 cm x 1 cm x 1 cm. Place the flour in a shallow dish. Divide the mince mixture into level tablespoon portions. Roll a portion into a long shape and flatten in the palm of your hand. Place the cheese in the centre and top with another portion of mince. Pinch the edges together and roll into a torpedo shape 6–7 cm long. Repeat with the remaining mince.
3. Heat the oil in a deep frying pan until a cube of bread dropped into the oil browns in 15 seconds. Toss half the meat patties in the flour, shake off the excess flour and fry for 3–5 minutes, or until browned all over and cooked through. Drain well on paper towels and repeat with the remaining meat patties. Serve hot.

NUTRITION PER SERVE
*Protein 9 g; Fat 8.5 g;
Carbohydrate 6.5 g; Dietary
Fibre 0.5 g; Cholesterol
50 mg; 580 kJ (140 cal)*

Note: Haloumi is a creamy white sheep's milk cheese kept in a brine. It can be bought from delicatessens and supermarkets.

Tabbouleh

Preparation time:
10 minutes +
30 minutes standing
Total cooking time:
Nil
Serves 4

3/4 cup (130 g) burghul
2 tomatoes, chopped
4 spring onions, finely
chopped
1 yellow capsicum,
finely chopped
1 1/2 cups (45 g) chopped
fresh flat-leaf parsley
1/4 cup (15 g) chopped
fresh mint
1/4 cup (60 ml) olive oil
1/4 cup (60 ml) lemon
juice
1 clove garlic, crushed

1. Cover the burghul with 3/4 cup (185 ml) boiling water. Leave for 30 minutes, or until the water is absorbed and the grains have swollen.
2. Combine the tomato, spring onion, capsicum, parsley, mint and burghul in a bowl. Season well.
3. Whisk together the oil, juice and garlic. Pour over the salad, toss and serve cold.

NUTRITION PER SERVE
*Protein 5 g; Fat 15 g;
Carbohydrate 20 g; Dietary
Fibre 7 g; Cholesterol
0 mg; 1025 kJ (245 cal)*

Note: Burghul is cracked wheat, also known as bulgar wheat.

*Meat patties with haloumi filling (top)
with Tabbouleh*

Marinated Olives

To ensure the olives store well, sterilise the jar first by rinsing it with boiling water, then place it in a warm oven until it is completely dry. For best results, these olives should be served at room temperature.

LEMON, GARLIC AND THYME
Cut 8 thin slices of lemon into quarters and put in a bowl with 1 1/2 teaspoons dried thyme leaves, 2 well-bruised cloves garlic, 250 g Kalamata olives and 250 g green olives. Spoon into a 1-litre sterilised jar with a lid and pour in about 1 3/4 cups (440 ml) olive oil, or enough to cover the olives completely. Seal and refrigerate for up to 3 months. Ready to eat in 2 days.

CHILLI, HERB AND LEMON
Combine 500 g cured black olives (these are the olives with a wrinkled appearance) with 2 teaspoons finely grated lemon rind, 2 teaspoons fresh oregano and 3 teaspoons dried chilli flakes. Transfer to a 3-cup (750 ml) sterilised jar with a lid and cover with olive oil. Seal and refrigerate for up to 3 months. Ready to eat after 2 days.

DILL, GARLIC AND ORANGE
In a bowl, combine 500 g Kalamata olives with 3 tablespoons coarsely chopped fresh dill, 1 bruised clove garlic, 4 thin slices of orange cut into eighths and 2 torn bay leaves. Spoon into a 1-litre sterilised jar with a lid and pour in about 1 3/4 cups (440 ml) olive oil or enough to cover the olives completely. Seal and refrigerate for up to 3 months. Ready to eat in 2 days.

From left to right: Coriander and orange; Chilli, herb and lemon; Lemon, garlic and thyme; Mixed olive pickles; 'A Sevilla'; Dill, garlic and orange.

MIXED OLIVE PICKLES

Combine 200 g jumbo green olives, 4 thickly sliced gherkins, 1 tablespoon capers, 2 quartered brown pickled onions, 2 teaspoons mustard seeds and 1 tablespoon fresh dill sprigs in a bowl. Spoon into a 2-cup (500 ml) sterilised jar with a lid and pour in 1/2 cup (125 ml) tarragon vinegar. Top with about 1/2 cup (125 ml) olive oil, or enough to cover completely. Seal and refrigerate for up to 3 months. Ready to eat after 2 days. Shake the jar occasionally.

'A SEVILLA'

Combine 1 tablespoon fresh rosemary leaves, 1 teaspoon dried thyme leaves, 1 torn bay leaf, 1 teaspoon lightly crushed fennel seeds, 2 well-bruised cloves garlic, 3 chopped anchovy fillets and 500 g stuffed green olives in a bowl. Spoon into a 1-litre sterilised jar with a lid and pour in 1/2 cup (125 ml) tarragon vinegar. Top with about 3/4 cup (185 ml) olive oil, or enough to completely. cover. Seal and refrigerate for up to 3 months. Ready to eat after 2 days. Shake the jar occasionally.

CORIANDER AND ORANGE

Lightly crush 2 teaspoons coriander seeds with a mortar and pestle. Combine the crushed coriander seeds, 1 teaspoon cumin seeds and 2 teaspoons grated orange rind in a bowl. Add 500 g jumbo green olives and mix together well. Spoon into a sterilised 1-litre jar with lid and pour in about 1 3/4 cups (440 ml) olive oil, or enough to completely cover the olives. Seal the jar and refrigerate for up to 3 months. Ready to eat after 2 days.

Baked sardines

Preparation time:
  30 minutes
Total cooking time:
  20 minutes
Serves 6

6 *fresh whole sardines*
1/4 cup (60 ml) olive oil
2 *tablespoons lemon*
  juice
1 *small clove garlic,*
  chopped
1 1/2 teaspoons dried
  oregano

1. Preheat the oven
to hot 210°C (415°F/
Gas 6–7). Clean the
sardines by scraping a
small knife along the
body of the sardine,
starting from the tail
end to remove any
scales (this is best done
under running water).
Make a slit along the
gut. Cut the head and
pull away slowly—the
intestines should come
away with the head.
Open the gut cavity and
clean away remaining
intestines. Pat dry and
drain on paper towels.
2. Put the sardines into
an ovenproof dish large
enough to fit them
snugly in one layer
and season with salt
and 1/2 teaspoon pepper.
Drizzle with oil and
lemon juice and sprinkle
with garlic and oregano.
Turn to coat and bake,
uncovered, in the top

half of the oven for
15–20 minutes, or until
the flesh flakes and
starts to come away
from the bone. Serve hot
or warm.

NUTRITION PER SERVE
Protein 2.5 g; Fat 10 g;
Carbohydrate 0.5 g; Dietary
Fibre 0 g; Cholesterol
15 mg; 115 kJ (48 cal)

Beetroot with skordalia

Preparation time:
  25 minutes
Total cooking time:
  1 hour
Serves 6–8

Skordalia
250 g floury potatoes,
  unpeeled
2 *cloves garlic, crushed*
1 *tablespoon white*
  wine vinegar
2 *tablespoons olive oil*

1 *kg beetroot, including*
  leaves
1/4 cup (60 ml) extra
  virgin olive oil
1 *tablespoon red wine*
  vinegar

1. Boil or steam the
potatoes until tender,
remove the peel and
mash. Cool, then mash
with the garlic, vinegar
and oil. Season well.
2. Cut the stems with
leaves from the beetroot

bulbs, leaving a 2 cm
stalk, and trim any
tough tops off the leaves.
Cut the whole leaf and
stem length into smaller
sections (halves or
thirds), and wash well.
3. Brush the bulbs to
remove any dirt. Bring
a large pan of water
to the boil, add the
unpeeled bulbs and
cook over high heat
for 20–40 minutes
(depending on bulb size),
or until tender when
pierced with a sharp
knife. Remove from the
pan with a slotted
spoon and cool slightly.
4. Return the cooking
water to the boil,
adding more water
if necessary. Add the
leaves and stems, and
boil for 8 minutes, or
until tender. Turn once
during cooking. Drain.
5. Put on a pair of
rubber gloves and peel
the skin from the bulbs.
Cut in half and then
into thick slices.
6. Arrange the leaves
and sliced bulbs on a
serving plate. Combine
the oil and vinegar and
season to taste. Drizzle
over the leaves and
bulbs, and serve the
skordalia on the side.

NUTRITION PER SERVE (8)
Protein 3 g; Fat 12 g;
Carbohydrate 15 g; Dietary
Fibre 4.5 g; Cholesterol
0 mg; 746 kJ (178 cal)

Baked sardines (top)
with Beetroot with skordalia

Lamb's liver with lemon

Preparation time:
  15 minutes
Total cooking time:
  10 minutes
Serves 6–8

500 g lamb's liver
1/4 cup (30 g) plain
  flour
1/2 teaspoon paprika
2 tablespoons olive oil
2 tablespoons lemon
  juice
1 teaspoon dried
  oregano

1. Wash the liver thoroughly, trim off any fatty deposits and cut into 2 cm thick slices. Cut the larger slices of liver in half or into thirds.
2. In a shallow dish, combine the flour and paprika and season with 1/2 teaspoon each of salt and cracked black pepper. Heat the oil in a frying pan over medium heat. Toss a third of the livers in the seasoned flour, shake off the excess flour and fry for 1 minute on each side or until browned, crusty and still pink inside. Drain on paper towels and place on warmed serving plate.

Repeat with the remaining slices of liver, cooking them in two batches. Cover with foil to keep warm.
3. Remove the pan from the heat and add the lemon juice—it should bubble in the hot pan. Allow the bubbles to subside, then pour the pan juices over the livers and sprinkle with oregano. Serve hot.

NUTRITION PER SERVE (8)
Protein 15 g; Fat 9.5 g; Carbohydrate 4.5 g; Dietary Fibre 0 g; Cholesterol 270 mg; 660 kJ (160 cal)

Eggplant salad

Preparation time:
  30 minutes +
  1 hour chilling
Total cooking time:
  1 hour
Serves 4–6

1 red capsicum
1 large eggplant, cut
  into four wedges
1/2 red onion, cut into
  thin wedges
1 medium tomato,
  chopped
1 tablespoon chopped
  fresh flat-leaf parsley
1 small clove garlic,
  crushed
3 teaspoons extra
  virgin olive oil
1 teaspoon red wine
  vinegar

1. Preheat the oven to moderately hot 200°C (400°F/Gas 6) and line a baking tray with foil.
2. Cut the capsicum into quarters and remove the seeds and the membrane. Place the capsicum skin-side-up and the eggplant on the baking tray. Bake for 50–60 minutes, or until the capsicum skin has blistered and the eggplant is browned and soft when pierced with a sharp knife.
3. Leave until cool enough to handle, then carefully remove the skins from both vegetables. Cut the capsicum into long thin strips and roughly chop the eggplant flesh. Place in a bowl with the onion, tomato, parsley and garlic. Whisk together the oil and vinegar in a small jug, and season with plenty of salt and cracked black pepper. Pour over the salad and mix well. Cover and refrigerate for 1 hour before serving.

NUTRITION PER SERVE (6)
Protein 1.5 g; Fat 2.5 g; Carbohydrate 2.5 g; Dietary Fibre 2 g; Cholesterol 0 mg; 170 kJ (40 cal)

Note: This recipe can be made a day ahead and stored in an airtight container in the refrigerator.

Lamb's liver with lemon (top)
with Eggplant salad

Fried whitebait

Preparation time:
  10 minutes
Total cooking time:
  10 minutes
Serves 6

500 g whitebait
2 teaspoons sea salt
1/3 cup (40 g) plain
  flour
1/4 cup (30 g) cornflour
2 teaspoons finely
  chopped fresh flat-leaf
  parsley
oil, for deep-frying
1 lemon, cut into
  wedges, for serving

1. Combine the whitebait and sea salt in a bowl and mix well. Cover and refrigerate.
2. Combine the sifted flours and parsley in a bowl and season well with cracked pepper. Fill a deep heavy-based pan one-third full of oil and heat until a cube of bread dropped into the oil browns in 15 seconds. Toss a third of the whitebait in the flour mixture, shake off the excess flour, and deep-fry for 1 1/2 minutes, or until pale and crisp. Drain well on crumpled paper towels. Repeat with the remaining whitebait, cooking in two batches.
3. Reheat the oil and fry the whitebait a second time in three batches for 1 minute each, or until lightly browned. Drain on paper towels and serve hot with lemon wedges.

NUTRITION PER SERVE
*Protein 20 g; Fat 9 g;
Carbohydrate 9.5 g; Dietary
Fibre 0.5 g; Cholesterol
60 mg; 795 kJ (190 cal)*

Deep-fried squid

Preparation time:
  30 minutes +
  30 minutes chilling
Total cooking time:
  5 minutes
Serves 4

480 g (about 18)
  small squid
1/3 cup (40 g) plain
  flour
oil, for deep-frying
1/2 lemon, cut into
  wedges, for serving

1. To clean the squid, gently pull the tentacles away from the hood—the intestines should come away with them. Remove the intestines from the tentacles by cutting under the eyes and remove the beak if it remains in the centre of the tentacles. Pull away the soft bone from the hood. Rub the hoods under running water and the skin should come away easily. Wash the hoods and tentacles and drain well. Place in a bowl and season well with salt. Cover and refrigerate for about 30 minutes.
2. Combine the flour with a pinch each of salt and cracked pepper in a shallow dish. Fill a deep heavy-based pan one-third full of oil and heat until a cube of bread dropped into the oil browns in 15 seconds. Coat the calamari hoods in flour and deep-fry in batches for about 30–60 seconds, or until lightly browned and tender. Toss the tentacles in the flour and deep-fry for 20–30 seconds, or until lightly browned and tender. Partially cover the deep-fryer while cooking as the squid tends to splatter. Drain on paper towels then transfer to a serving platter, sprinkle with salt and serve hot with lemon wedges.

NUTRITION PER SERVE
*Protein 20 g; Fat 11 g;
Carbohydrate 7.5 g; Dietary
Fibre 0.5 g; Cholesterol
240 mg; 905 kJ (215 cal)*

Note: Cleaned squid are sometimes available from fishmongers.

*Fried whitebait (top)
with Deep-fried squid*

Remove the eyes by cutting a round of flesh from the base of the head.

Carefully slit open the head and remove the gut.

Octopus in red wine

Preparation time:
45 minutes
Total cooking time:
2 hours 20 minutes
Serves 4

1 kg small octopus
2 tablespoons olive oil
180 g small brown
 pickling onions
1/3 cup (80 ml) red wine
 vinegar
3/4 cup (185 ml) dry red
 wine
1 ripe tomato, halved,
 grated and skin
 discarded
1 bay leaf
1 teaspoon dried
 oregano leaves

1. To clean the octopus, use a small sharp knife and remove the head from the tentacles. Remove the eyes by cutting a round of flesh from the base of the head. To clean the head, carefully slit open the head and remove the gut. Cut the head in half. Push out the beak from the centre of the tentacles. Cut the tentacles into sets of four or two, depending on the size of the octopus. Pull away the skin from the head and tentacles if it comes away easily.
2. Place the octopus in a large pan and cook over high heat in its own liquid for 15–20 minutes, or until dry. Add the oil and the onions, and toss over heat until well coated. Add the vinegar, wine, tomato, bay leaf, oregano, 1 cup (250 ml) water and 1/2 teaspoon cracked black pepper and bring to the boil. Reduce the heat to low and simmer for 1 1/2 to 2 hours, or until the octopus is tender. If the octopus is not yet tender, add a little more water and continue cooking. The liquid remaining in the pan should just coat the octopus like a sauce. Delicious served hot with crusty bread.

NUTRITION PER SERVE
Protein 42 g; Fat 13 g; Carbohydrate 6.5 g; Dietary Fibre 1 g; Cholesterol 498 mg; 1314 kJ (315 cal)

Note: When choosing octopus, select those that are younger and smaller, as they will be more tender than the larger ones.
Variation: The octopus is closely related to squid and cuttlefish, so if you are unable to buy small octopus, either of these can be substituted.
Hint: Choose a ripe, but still firm, tomato to make grating easier.

Octopus in red wine

Use your fingers to push out the beak from the centre of the tentacles.

Cook the octopus in its own liquid over high heat until dry.

Pan-fried cheese

Preparation time:
  10 minutes
Total cooking time:
  5 minutes
Serves 2–3

250 g kefalograviera
  (see Note)
2 tablespoons plain
  flour
1/4 cup (60 ml) olive
  oil
1/2 teaspoon dried
  oregano
1/2 lemon cut into
  wedges, for serving

1. Cut the cheese into 1 cm slices. The pieces can be as large as you wish, as they can be cut smaller for serving.
2. Put the flour in a shallow dish and season well with cracked pepper. Toss the cheese in the flour.
3. Heat the oil over high heat in a frying pan until hot. Add the cheese to the pan and cook for 1 minute, or until browned and crusty underneath. Using an egg slice, carefully turn the cheese to brown the other side. Lift onto a serving plate and sprinkle with oregano. Serve hot with lemon wedges, squeezing lemon juice over the top. Ideally served with fresh bread.

Note: Kefalograviera and kefalotyri are pale hard sheep's milk cheeses originating in Greece.

NUTRITION PER SERVE (3)
Protein 35 g; Fat 45 g; Carbohydrate 6 g; Dietary Fibre 0.5 g; Cholesterol 80 mg; 2370 kJ (565 cal)

Pickled octopus

Preparation time:
  30 minutes +
  1–2 days chilling
Total cooking time:
  1 hour
Serves 4–6

1 kg small octopus
12 whole black
  peppercorns
2 bay leaves
1 tablespoon fresh
  oregano
2 teaspoons fresh
  thyme
1 small clove garlic,
  thinly sliced
1 cup (250 ml) red
  wine vinegar
1 1/3 cups (350 ml)
  olive oil

1. To clean the octopus, use a small sharp knife and remove the head from the tentacles. Remove the eyes by cutting a round of flesh from the base of the head. Carefully slit open the head and remove the gut. Cut the head in half. Push out the beak from the centre of the tentacles. Cut the tentacles into sets of two. Pull away the skin from the head and tentacles if it comes away easily.
2. Put the octopus, peppercorns and bay leaves in a pan and cook, covered, over medium–low heat in its own liquid for 1 hour, or until tender. Drain and cool for 20 minutes. Reserve the peppercorns and bay leaves.
3. Sterilise a 1-litre glass jar by rinsing with boiling water and drying in a warm oven. Place the octopus, peppercorns and bay leaves into the jar. Add the herbs and garlic, and pour in the vinegar and enough of the oil to completely cover the octopus, so that it doesn't break the surface. Seal and gently shake the jar to mix the ingredients.
4. Refrigerate for 1–2 days, shaking the jar occasionally. Store in the refrigerator for up to 5 days. Return to room temperature before serving.

NUTRITION PER SERVE (6)
Protein 30 g; Fat 15 g; Carbohydrate 0 g; Dietary Fibre 0 g; Cholesterol 330 mg; 1045 kJ (250 cal)

Pan-fried cheese (top) with Pickled octopus

Olive oil biscuits

Preparation time:
  30 minutes +
  1 hour 30 minutes
  standing
Total cooking time:
  1 hour 30 minutes
Makes about 45

7 g dried yeast
1 teaspoon sugar
1 1/2 cups (185 g) plain
  white flour
1 1/2 cups (225 g) plain
  wholemeal flour
1 teaspoon ground
  cinnamon
1 1/2 tablespoons
  sesame seeds, toasted
1/2 cup (125 ml) olive oil

Topping
4 ripe tomatoes, diced
160 g feta, crumbled
1/3 cup (80 ml) extra
  virgin olive oil
2 tablespoons red wine
  vinegar
1 teaspoon dried
  oregano

1. Combine the yeast, sugar, 2 tablespoons of the white flour and 1/4 cup (60 ml) warm water in a bowl. Cover with plastic wrap and leave in a warm place for 10 minutes, or until frothy.
2. Sift the remaining flours and cinnamon in a large bowl, return the husks to the bowl and stir through the sesame seeds and 1/2 teaspoon salt. Pour in the oil and rub it in by lifting the flour mixture onto one hand and lightly rubbing the other hand over the top. Make a well in the centre and add the yeast mixture and about 1/4 cup (60 ml) warm water, or enough to mix to a soft but not sticky dough.
3. Knead on a floured surface for about 2 minutes, or until smooth and elastic. Place in a lightly oiled bowl, turning the dough to coat in the oil. Cover loosely with plastic wrap and leave in a warm place for 45–60 minutes, or until doubled in bulk.
4. Lightly grease an oven tray. Punch down the dough and divide it into three portions and roll each on a lightly floured surface into a long sausage shape about 30 cm long. Place the first roll onto the tray. Cut through almost to the base of the roll at 2 cm intervals with a serrated knife (about 15 portions). Repeat with remaining rolls.
5. Cover with a tea towel and leave in a warm place for 30 minutes, or until well risen. Preheat the oven to moderately hot 200°C (400°F/Gas 6). Bake for 30 minutes, or until browned underneath and the rolls sound hollow when tapped. Reduce the temperature to very slow 120°C (250°F/Gas 1/2). Cool on the tray for 5 minutes.
6. Transfer each roll to a cutting board and cut through the markings. Place cut-side-up on two oven trays. Bake for 30 minutes, or until the top feels dry. Turn each biscuit and bake for a further 30 minutes, or until completely dry and crisp. Cool. Store in an airtight container for up to 3 weeks.
7. Dunk each biscuit quickly into cold water and place on a tray. Top with the combined tomato and feta. Drizzle on the combined oil and vinegar and sprinkle with oregano. Season.

NUTRITION PER SERVE
Protein 1.5 g; Fat 5.5 g; Carbohydrate 4 g; Dietary Fibre 0.5 g; Cholesterol 2.5 mg; 300 kJ (70 cal)

Variation: For a different topping, combine 10 pitted and quartered Kalamata olives, 1 sliced roasted capsicum and 2 tablespoons chopped flat-leaf parsley. Season. Drizzle on 3 tablespoons extra virgin olive oil and 1 tablespoon red wine vinegar, combined.

Olive oil biscuits

Barbecued haloumi

Preparation time:
15 minutes
Total cooking time:
10 minutes
Makes 10

1 French bread stick
250 g haloumi (see
   Note)
3 tablespoons olive oil
1 clove garlic, crushed
$^1/2$ teaspoon finely
   chopped fresh mint

1. Cut the bread diagonally into $1^1/2$ cm slices. Cut the haloumi into the same number of 3–5 mm thick slices to fit the slice of bread.
2. Heat a lightly oiled barbecue plate until hot. Barbecue the bread on both sides until well browned and place onto a serving plate. Brush lightly with 1 tablespoon olive oil.
3. Brush the haloumi with 1 tablespoon olive oil and the garlic, and barbecue for 1 minute or until soft and browned on both sides. Lift with an egg slice onto the bread, drizzle with the remaining oil and sprinkle with mint and pepper. Serve hot.

NUTRITION PER PIECE
*Protein 6.5 g; Fat 10 g;
Carbohydrate 7.5 g; Dietary
Fibre 0.5 g; Cholesterol
13 mg; 620 kJ (150 cal)*

Note: Haloumi is a creamy white sheep's milk cheese kept in a brine. It can be bought in vacuum-packed packets or in bulk from delicatessens or most supermarkets.

Lima bean casserole

Preparation time:
20 minutes +
   overnight soaking
Total cooking time:
2 hours
Serves 6–8

1 cup (185 g) dried
   lima beans
$^1/4$ cup (60 ml) olive oil
1 large onion, halved
   and sliced
1 clove garlic, chopped
1 small carrot, chopped
1 small stick celery,
   chopped
400 g can crushed
   tomatoes
1 tablespoon tomato
   paste
2 teaspoons chopped
   fresh dill

1. Cover the lima beans with plenty of cold water and leave overnight. Drain well.
2. Bring a large pan of water to the boil, add the beans and return to the boil, then reduce the heat to medium and cook, partially covered, for 45–60 minutes, or until the beans are tender but not mushy. Drain. Preheat the oven to moderate 180°C (350°F/Gas 4).
3. Heat the oil in a flameproof 2.5 litre casserole over medium heat. Add the onion, garlic, carrot and celery, and cook for 5 minutes, or until the onion is translucent. Add the crushed tomatoes, tomato paste and $^1/2$ cup (125 ml) water. Bring to the boil, then reduce the heat and simmer for 3 minutes.
4. Add the lima beans and dill, and season to taste with salt and cracked pepper. Bring back to the boil, then transfer to the oven and bake, uncovered, for 50 minutes, or until thick and the beans are soft. Serve hot or at room temperature.

NUTRITION PER SERVE (8)
*Protein 6 g; Fat 7.5 g;
Carbohydrate 10 g; Dietary
Fibre 5.5 g; Cholesterol
0 mg; 590 kJ (140 cal)*

Note: Lima bean casserole can be made up to 3 days ahead and kept covered in the refrigerator. Return to room temperature before serving.

*Barbecued haloumi (top)
with Lima bean casserole*

Dips and Spreads

No meze feast would be complete without some of the delicious dips Mediterranean cuisine is famous for.

TARAMASALATA

Remove the crusts from 4 slices of white bread. Put the bread in a bowl, cover with water, drain and squeeze out as much water as possible, and place in a medium bowl. Finely grate a small onion into the bowl and add 100 g tarama (cod roe), 2 tablespoons freshly squeezed lemon juice, 3 tablespoons olive oil and a pinch of black pepper. Mix with a fork until well combined. Alternatively, process the ingredients until smooth. Can be made up to 3 days ahead and stored in an airtight container in the refrigerator. Makes about 1 cup (250 ml).

FETA SPREAD

Place 100 g ricotta, 175 g feta, 3 tablespoons olive oil, 3 teaspoons finely chopped fresh mint and $1/4$ teaspoon cracked black pepper in a bowl. Mix with a fork to mash the cheeses, yet still retain a lumpy texture. Can be made up to 3 days ahead and stored in an airtight container in the refrigerator. Makes about 1 cup (250 ml).

BABA GANOUJ

Make four shallow slits in a large (500 g) eggplant, then grill or barbecue for 15–20 minutes, turning to char on all sides until the eggplant is completely soft. Transfer to a colander and drain well. Allow to cool, then peel and roughly chop the eggplant and place in a food processor with $1^1/2$ tablespoons freshly squeezed lemon juice, $1^1/2$ tablespoons olive oil, 2 tablespoons tahini paste, 2 cloves crushed garlic, $1/2$ teaspoon ground cumin, and a good pinch each of salt and cracked black pepper. Process until smooth, transfer to a bowl and stir through $1/4$ cup (7 g) chopped fresh flat-leaf parsley. Can be made up to 3 days ahead and stored in an airtight container in the refrigerator. Makes about 1 cup (250 ml).

HUMMUS

Soak 125 g dried chickpeas overnight in plenty of water. Drain and transfer to a pan of boiling water. Cook, covered, over medium heat for 1 hour, or until tender. Drain and return to the pan. Add 1 tablespoon olive oil, 1 small finely chopped onion, 1 1/2 teaspoons ground cumin and a pinch of cayenne pepper to the pan and cook over high heat for 1 minute, or until aromatic. Place in a food processor and add 2 tablespoons freshly squeezed lemon juice, 1/2 cup (125 ml) olive oil and 3 crushed cloves garlic. Season with salt and process until smooth. Serve as is or add water if you prefer a thinner consistency. Can be made up to 5 days ahead and stored in an airtight container in the refrigerator. Makes about 2 cups (500 ml).

RED CAPSICUM AND WALNUT DIP

Quarter and seed 2 red capsicums. Place skin-side-up under a preheated grill and grill until the skin is blistered. Remove the skin. Heat 1 tablespoon olive oil in a pan, add 1 chopped onion and 1 crushed clove garlic and cook until soft. Stir in 1/2 teaspoon dried chilli flakes. Process 1/2 cup (60 g) walnuts until fine and add the capsicum, the onion mixture, 3 tablespoons olive oil, 2 teaspoons red wine vinegar and 1/4 teaspoon salt. Process until fine and almost smooth. Can be made up to 5 days ahead and stored in an airtight container in the refrigerator. Makes about 1 cup (250 ml).

TZATZIKI

Coarsely grate 1 unpeeled small green cucumber into a bowl. Add 1 cup (250 ml) thick Greek-style yoghurt, 2 crushed cloves garlic, 1 tablespoon red wine vinegar, 1 tablespoon olive oil, 1/4 teaspoon salt and 1/2 teaspoon cracked black pepper. Mix together well and serve. Can be made up to 3 days ahead and stored in an airtight container in the refrigerator. Makes about 1 1/2 cups (375 ml).

Opposite page
From top to bottom: Taramasalata; Feta spread; Baba ganouj.
This page
From top to bottom: Hummus; Red capsicum and walnut dip; Tzatziki.

Pickled cauliflower

Preparation time:
  10 minutes
Total cooking time:
  10 minutes
Serves 4–6

2 cups (500 ml) white
  wine vinegar
1 tablespoon yellow
  mustard seeds
1/2 teaspoon cumin
  seeds
3 bay leaves
3/4 cup (185 g) caster
  sugar
400 g cauliflower, cut
  into florets

1. Put the vinegar,
mustard seeds, cumin
seeds, bay leaves and
sugar into a pan. Stir
over medium heat
until the sugar has
dissolved. Bring to the
boil, then reduce the
heat and add the
cauliflower. Simmer for
4 minutes, or until just
tender, but still firm.
2. Remove from the
heat and leave the
cauliflower to cool in
the liquid. Serve chilled
or at room temperature.

NUTRITION PER SERVE (6)
*Protein 1.5 g; Fat 0 g;
Carbohydrate 30 g; Dietary
Fibre 1 g; Cholesterol
0 mg; 600 kJ (145 cal)*

Note: To store, rinse a
clean glass jar with a
lid with boiling water

and dry in a warm
oven. Put the hot liquid
and cauliflower in the
jar, seal while hot
and keep for up to
3 months unopened.

Saffron risotto-stuffed baby squid

Preparation time:
  40 minutes +
  20 minutes cooling
Total cooking time:
  20 minutes
Makes 16

1/4 cup (60 ml) dry
  white wine
2 cups (500 ml)
  vegetable stock
1/2 fennel bulb
1 leek, white part only
25 g butter
1 tablespoon vegetable
  oil
1 cup (220 g) arborio
  rice
pinch of ground saffron
16 baby squid hoods
  (approximately
  35 g each)
3 lemons, sliced

1. Combine the wine
and stock in a pan and
bring to a simmer over
medium heat.
2. Cut the fennel and
leek into thin slices and
place in a heavy-based
pan with the butter and
oil. Cook, stirring, over
medium heat for

4 minutes, or until
softened. Add the rice
and stir for 1 minute.
Gradually add the hot
stock mixture, a ladle
at a time, stirring
frequently until all
the liquid has been
absorbed before adding
more. When the rice is
tender add the saffron
and season well with
salt and cracked
pepper. Spread the
risotto onto a flat tray
to cool slightly.
3. Stuff each squid with
2 teaspoons of risotto.
Be careful not to
overfill the squid or
it may split during
cooking. Secure the top
of each squid with a
toothpick. Preheat the
oven to moderate
180°C (350°F/Gas 4).
4. Line a baking tray
with foil, add the
lemon slices and top
with the stuffed squid.
Cover and bake for
20 minutes, or until the
squid are cooked and
tender, turning once.
Don't spoon the sauce
over the squid as it is
too bitter. Discard the
lemon and juices after
cooking, and serve the
squid whole or cut
into slices.

NUTRITION PER SERVE
*Protein 1.5 g; Fat 2.5 g;
Carbohydrate 12 g; Dietary
Fibre 1 g; Cholesterol
8.5 mg; 340 kJ (80 cal)*

*Pickled cauliflower (top)
with Saffron risotto-stuffed baby squid*

Stewed artichokes

Preparation time:
15 minutes
Total cooking time:
10 minutes
Serves 4

2 x 400 g cans globe
artichokes, drained
10 strips preserved
*lemon, flesh removed
and peel washed*
*1/2 cup (125 ml) olive
oil*
*1/2 cup (125 ml)
vegetable oil*
*1/2 cup (125 ml) sherry
vinegar*
1 tablespoon fresh
lemon thyme leaves

1. Put the artichokes,
peel, oils, vinegar and
thyme in a pan with a
lid. Cover and gently
simmer for 10 minutes.
Remove from the heat
and cool the artichokes
in the liquid.
2. Serve warm or cold
by themselves, or as an
accompaniment to
grilled lamb pieces.

NUTRITION PER SERVE
*Protein 4 g; Fat 15 g;
Carbohydrate 3 g; Dietary
Fibre 6 g; Cholesterol
0 mg; 680 kJ (162 cal)*

Note: To successfully
store the artichokes,
sterilise the jar first by
rinsing with boiling

water and drying in a
warm oven. Pour the
artichokes and juice
into the jar while still
hot. Keep for up to
3 months unopened.
Note: Preserved lemons
are fresh lemons
preserved in salt, and
are available from
speciality food stores.

Mussel salad with saffron dressing

Preparation time:
40 minutes
Total cooking time:
30 minutes
Serves 4–6

250 g kipfler potatoes,
unpeeled
20 black mussels
*1/3 cup (80 ml) dry
white wine*
1 small onion, sliced
2 sprigs fresh thyme
2 bay leaves
*pinch of powdered
saffron*
2 tablespoons sour
cream
1 teaspoon chopped
fresh parsley

1. Place the potatoes in
a pan of cold, lightly
salted water. Bring to
the boil, then reduce
the heat and simmer
for 20 minutes, or until
tender. Drain and cool.

2. Remove the beards
from the mussels and
scrub the shells. Discard
any mussels that don't
close when tapped.
Place the wine, onion,
thyme sprigs, bay leaves
and half the mussels in
a pot with a tight-fitting
lid. Cover and cook
over high heat, stirring
once, for about
4 minutes, or until the
mussels start to open.
Take the mussels out of
the pot with tongs as
they open, making sure
any unopened mussels
are discarded. Cook
the remaining mussels
the same way, and
leave to cool.
3. Strain the mussel
cooking liquid, and
reserve 1/4 cup (60 ml)
of the liquid. While the
liquid is still warm, stir
in the saffron. Whisk
in the sour cream and
season well with salt
and cracked pepper.
4. Slice the potatoes
on the diagonal into
2 cm slices. Remove
the mussels from their
shell and discard the
shells. Arrange the
potato slices and
mussels on a serving
plate and pour on
the saffron dressing.
Sprinkle with chopped
parsley and serve
immediately.

NUTRITION PER SERVE (6)
*Protein 1.5 g; Fat 4.5 g;
Carbohydrate 6.5 g; Dietary
Fibre 1 g; Cholesterol
8.5 mg; 645 kJ (153 cal)*

---

*Stewed artichokes (top)
with Mussel salad with saffron dressing*

White fish salad with orange

Preparation time:
  30 minutes
Total cooking time:
  5 minutes
Serves 4

500 g firm white fish
  cutlets
2 tablespoons sherry
  vinegar
1 tablespoon orange
  juice
1 tablespoon olive oil
2 oranges
1/2 fennel bulb, thinly
  sliced
1/2 cup (80 g)
  marinated black
  olives

1. Remove the skin and bones from the cutlets. You will need about 250 g fish flesh, cut into large chunks (about 5 cm).
2. To make the vinegar dressing, mix together the vinegar, orange juice and olive oil, and season with salt and cracked black pepper.
3. In a pan, bring some lightly salted water to a simmer and gently place the fish into the water. Cook for 5 minutes, or until just cooked. Using a slotted spoon, carefully remove the fish from the water and, while still warm, cut into fine pieces. Add the fish pieces to the vinegar dressing and allow to cool.
4. Remove the skin and bitter white pith from the oranges. Using a small sharp knife, cut between the membranes to remove the orange segments.
5. In a bowl, toss together the slices of fennel, olives and orange segments, then spoon the fish mixture over the top of the salad. Season to taste with salt and cracked pepper. Serve at room temperature.

NUTRITION PER SERVE
*Protein 25 g; Fat 4.3 g;
Carbohydrate 6 g; Dietary
Fibre 2 g; Cholesterol
90 mg; 730 kJ (175 cal)*

Souvlakia

Preparation time:
  20 minutes +
  1 hour soaking +
  1 hour chilling
Total cooking time:
  10 minutes
Serves 4–6

1 kg boneless pork loin
  steak
1 tablespoon dried
  oregano
1/2 cup (125 ml) lemon
  juice
2 cloves garlic, crushed
1 tablespoon lemon
  juice, extra
1 tablespoon olive oil

1. Soak twelve 15 cm wooden skewers in water for 1 hour, or until they sink. This will ensure they don't burn during cooking.
2. Trim the pork steaks and cut them into 2 cm cubes. Put the oregano, lemon juice, garlic and 1/2 teaspoon cracked black pepper in a bowl. Add the pork, stir until well coated, then cover and refrigerate for 1 hour. Whisk the extra lemon juice, oil, 1/2 teaspoon salt and 1/2 teaspoon cracked black pepper in a small jug until well combined.
3. Thread the pork onto the prepared skewers.
4. Heat a lightly oiled barbecue hot plate until hot or heat a grill to its highest setting. Cook the souvlakia for 8–10 minutes, turning once during cooking. Place on a serving platter and pour the whisked lemon mixture over the top. Serve hot with tzatziki (page 49).

NUTRITION PER SERVE (6)
*Protein 40 g; Fat 6 g;
Carbohydrate 0.5 g; Dietary
Fibre 0 g; Cholesterol
80 mg; 885 kJ (210 cal)*

Note: The flavours will be enhanced if you marinate the pork a few hours ahead.

White fish salad with orange (top) with Souvlakia

Chop the bacon and mushrooms into small dice.

Cook the bacon and mushroom until tender and season well.

Borek of mushroom

Preparation time:
  40 minutes + cooling
Total cooking time:
  30 minutes per batch
Makes 24

4 rashers bacon
250 g mushrooms
1 tablespoon olive oil
1 onion, chopped
1/4 teaspoon paprika
6 sheets ready-rolled
  puff pastry, thawed

1. Chop the bacon and mushrooms into 1/2 cm cubes. Heat the olive oil in a non-stick frying pan over medium heat, and add the chopped onion and paprika. Fry the onion for 3 minutes without browning. Add the bacon and cook for a further 3 minutes. Add the mushroom and cook for 5 minutes more, or until all of the ingredients in the pan are tender. Season with plenty of salt and cracked black pepper, then spoon the mixture into a bowl. Set aside and allow to cool completely.
2. Using a 10 cm pastry cutter, cut four rounds out of each sheet of defrosted pastry. Place the rounds in the refrigerator to make handling them easier. Preheat the oven to moderately hot 200°C (400°F/Gas 6).
3. Spoon 1 tablespoon of the cold bacon and mushroom mixture into the centre of each round of pastry. Draw up the pastry to form four sides. To seal the borek, pinch the sides together firmly with wet fingertips. Repeat with the remaining pastry and filling.

4. Bake the borek on an oven tray covered with baking paper for 20–30 minutes, or until the pastry is golden and cooked. These borek are delicious eaten straight from the oven or served warm.

NUTRITION PER SERVE
Protein 5.5 g; Fat 10 g; Carbohydrate 15 g; Dietary Fibre 1 g; Cholesterol 18 mg; 760 kJ (180 cal)

Note: Although borek are traditionally thought to be of Turkish origin, they are also made in the Middle East and Eastern Europe. They are not always filled with mushroom; variations include meat, spinach and cheese, and the borek can be shaped into triangles, squares and circles. The pastry can also vary—shortcrust or filo pastry, or leavened dough can be substituted for the puff pastry if preferred.

Borek of mushroom

Spoon tablespoons of the mixture into the centre of each pastry round.

Draw up the pastry to form four sides and pinch the sides together to seal.

Cinnamon beef in cabbage leaves

Preparation time:
 1 hour
Total cooking time:
 20 minutes
Makes 8

1 tablespoon oil
2 onions, chopped
400 g beef mince
1/4 teaspoon ground
 nutmeg
1 teaspoon ground
 cinnamon
1/3 cup (50 g) pine nuts,
 lightly roasted
1 tablespoon chopped
 fresh parsley
1 tablespoon chopped
 fresh mint
8 large cabbage leaves

1. Heat the oil in a non-stick frying pan and fry the onions until soft. Add the beef mince, nutmeg, cinnamon and pine nuts. Season well with salt and cracked pepper. Cook for 5 minutes, or until the meat is cooked. Transfer to a bowl and cool. Stir in the parsley and mint.
2. Bring a large pan of lightly salted water to the boil. Put the cabbage leaves into the pan a few at a time and cook for 2 minutes, or until just tender, then run them under cold water. Cut out the thick stems with scissors.
3. Place spoonfuls of the mince mixture on each cabbage leaf and roll up, tucking in the sides of the leaves to form a parcel so that the filling is completely enclosed. Steam the rolls in a steamer over a pan of simmering water for 10 minutes, or until heated through. Serve warm or cold.

NUTRITION PER SERVE
Protein 12 g; Fat 12 g; Carbohydrate 2 g; Dietary Fibre 1.5 g; Cholesterol 30 mg; 685 kJ (165 cal)

White gazpacho

Preparation time:
 45 minutes +
 overnight chilling
Total cooking time:
 2 minutes
Serves 4

1/2 cup (125 ml)
 chicken stock
1 slice bread, crust
 removed, diced
1 2/3 cups (300 g) large
 green grapes
1/2 cup (95 g) ground
 almonds
1 clove garlic, crushed
1/3 cup (80 ml) olive oil
1 1/2 tablespoons verjus
 or lemon juice (see
 Note)
green grapes, peeled,
 to garnish

1. In a small pan, heat the chicken stock and add the diced bread. Using a fork, mash the bread into the stock until all the liquid has been absorbed and the bread is soft. Cool.
2. In a food processor, purée the grapes and strain to remove skins and seeds. Place the ground almonds, garlic and bread in the cleaned food processor. With the motor running on low speed, gradually pour in the grape purée and olive oil. Season to taste. Strain through a fine strainer if you prefer a smoother texture. Add the verjus or lemon juice to freshen the soup.
3. Chill the soup completely and serve cold with sliced green grapes on the top. If the soup is too thick, add a little more chicken stock. For best results, leave the soup in the refrigerator overnight. Small servings are recommended as this dish is quite rich.

NUTRITION PER SERVE
Protein 6 g; Fat 35 g; Carbohydrate 15 g; Dietary Fibre 3 g; Cholesterol 0 mg; 1580 kJ (375 cal)

Note: Verjus is a sour liquid made mainly from unripe grapes.

Cinnamon beef in cabbage leaves (top)
with White gazpacho

Tuna skewers with caperberries

Preparation time:
 20 minutes +
 1 hour soaking +
 30 minutes marinating
Total cooking time:
 10 minutes
Makes 8

250 g piece raw tuna
1/2 lemon
1 tablespoon lemon
 juice
1 tablespoon olive oil
16 caperberries
8 green olives, stuffed
 with an anchovy fillet

1. If you are using
wooden skewers, soak
them in cold water for
1 hour, or until they
sink, to stop them
burning while grilling.
Cut the tuna into
24 even-sized cubes.
Remove the rind from
the lemon, avoiding the
bitter white pith, and
cut into thin strips.
Combine the tuna,
lemon rind, lemon
juice and oil in a bowl.
2. Thread 3 pieces of
tuna, 2 caperberries
and 1 stuffed olive onto
each skewer alternating
each ingredient
(that is, 1 piece of tuna,
1 caperberry, 1 tuna,
1 olive and so on).
3. Lay the tuna skewers

in a non-metallic dish
and pour on the lemon
marinade. Refrigerate,
covered, for 30 minutes.
4. Under a preheated
grill, grill the tuna
skewers for 1 minute
on each side (there
should be four sides
to your tuna) for a total
of 4 minutes, or until
the tuna is cooked to
your liking. Do not
overcook or the tuna
will dry out. Serve hot.

NUTRITION PER SKEWER
*Protein 3 g; Fat 5 g;
Carbohydrate 35 g; Dietary
Fibre 0.5 g; Cholesterol
0 mg; 305 kJ (73 cal)*

Cheese pastries

Preparation time:
 40 minutes
Total cooking time:
 20 minutes
Makes 16

160 g feta, grated
60 g ricotta
2 tablespoons chopped
 fresh mint
1 egg, lightly beaten
2 spring onions, finely
 chopped
2 tablespoons dry
 breadcrumbs
4 sheets ready-rolled
 puff pastry
1 egg, extra, lightly
 beaten
1 tablespoon sesame
 seeds

1. Preheat the oven
to hot 220°C (425°F/
Gas 7). Lightly grease
two baking trays.
2. Put the grated feta,
ricotta, mint, beaten
egg, spring onion,
breadcrumbs and
1/2 teaspoon cracked
black pepper in a bowl
and mix with a fork to
combine and break up
the ricotta.
3. Using a 10 cm
pastry cutter or saucer,
cut rounds from the
pastry sheets. Spoon
level tablespoons of the
cheese mixture into
the centre of each
round and lightly
brush the edges with
water. Fold over to
enclose the filling,
expelling any air, and
firmly seal with the
prongs of a fork to
form a crescent shape.
Brush with the extra
egg and sprinkle with
sesame seeds.
4. Put the crescents
on the baking trays and
bake for 15–20 minutes,
or until the pastry is
well browned and
puffed. Should be
served hot.

NUTRITION PER PASTRY
*Protein 5.5 g; Fat 15 g;
Carbohydrate 15 g; Dietary
Fibre 0.5 g; Cholesterol
40 mg; 870 kJ (205 cal)*

Note: The pastries can
be prepared up to the
end of step 3 two days
ahead and kept, covered,
in the refrigerator.

*Tuna skewers with caperberries (top)
with Cheese pastries*

Green bean casserole

Preparation time:
25 minutes
Total cooking time:
35 minutes
Serves 6

500 g green beans
1/4 cup (60 ml) olive oil
2 onions, chopped
1 clove garlic, chopped
3 tomatoes, diced
1 tablespoon tomato paste
1/2 cup (125 ml) tomato purée
2 tablespoons chopped fresh flat-leaf parsley
1/4 teaspoon sugar

1. Top and tail the beans, then cut in half.
2. Heat the oil in a large pan and cook the onion and garlic over low heat for 5 minutes, or until soft. Add the tomatoes, paste and purée, and cook over medium heat for 5 minutes.
3. Add the beans, parsley and sugar. Season well with salt and pepper. Stir until the beans are well coated, then cook, covered, over low heat for 25 minutes, or until the beans are tender, stirring three to four times. Delicious served hot or at room temperature.

NUTRITION PER SERVE
Protein 3.5 g; Fat 10 g; Carbohydrate 7 g; Dietary Fibre 4 g; Cholesterol 0 mg; 545 kJ (130 cal)

Rice-stuffed tomatoes

Preparation time:
40 minutes
Total cooking time:
50 minutes
Makes 8

8 medium tomatoes
1/2 cup (110 g) short-grain rice
2 tablespoons olive oil
1 red onion, chopped
1 clove garlic, crushed
1 teaspoon dried oregano leaves
1/4 cup (40 g) pine nuts
1/4 cup (35 g) currants
1/2 cup (30 g) chopped fresh basil
2 tablespoons chopped fresh parsley
1 tablespoon chopped fresh dill
olive oil, to brush

1. Lightly oil a large baking dish. Preheat the oven to warm 160°C (315°F/Gas 2–3). Slice the top off each tomato and reserve the tops. Spoon out the flesh into a bowl, place into a strainer to drain the juice and then finely dice the flesh. Reserve the juice and pulp in separate bowls. Drain the tomato shells upside-down on a rack.
2. Boil the rice in a pan of lightly salted water for 10–12 minutes, or until just tender. Drain and set aside to cool.
3. Heat the olive oil in a frying pan. Fry the onion, garlic and oregano for 8 minutes, or until the onion is tender. Add the pine nuts and currants and cook for a further 5 minutes, stirring frequently. Remove from the heat and stir in the basil, parsley and dill. Season to taste.
4. Add the onion mixture and reserved tomato pulp to the rice and mix well. Fill the tomato shells with the rice mixture, piling it up over the top. Spoon 1 tablespoon of the reserved tomato juice on top of each tomato and replace the tomato tops.
5. Lightly brush the tomatoes with the olive oil. Arrange them in a baking dish. Bake for about 20–30 minutes, or until cooked and heated through. Serve warm or cold.

NUTRITION PER SERVE
Protein 3 g; Fat 10 g; Carbohydrate 15 g; Dietary Fibre 2.5 g; Cholesterol 0 mg; 695 kJ (165 cal)

Green bean casserole (top) with Rice-stuffed tomatoes

Index